Halah is a young Saudi female who holds a Master of Business Administration with honors from Alfaisal University, Riyadh, KSA. Her undergrad degree is in Business Science, specialized in management, international business and marketing with honors from the University of New Haven, Connecticut, USA, while enlisted on the dean's list.

Halah is a VP of Admin and Finance in a private company, and a certified PMP. She originally started her career as an investment officer then a wealth manager in SHB. Later on, she became a member of the founding team of Alinma Bank in retail banking group, contributed to the launch in the Kingdom of Saudi Arabia and assigned as a branch manager.

Halah's writing hobby has led her to articulate her passionate understanding of the world around her, and later joined *Arab News* (SRPC) for some time as a freelance feature writer, focused on Vision 2030 initiatives. She is a curious learner who self-indulges in enhancement of human capital, and fond of individual and organizational transformational practices, and she feels lucky to have worked with many dynamic people.

To my parents, who are the primary source of my core values and learnings, who encouraged me in every step of the way to aspire to master whatever I do without compromising my values.

To my parents, who are a crucial source of my values.

Halah Omar AlShathri

VALUES OF MASTERY

How Core Values Drive Individuals and Organizations to Perform with Mastery

AUSTIN MACAULEY PUBLISHERS®
LONDON * CAMBRIDGE * NEW YORK * SHARJAH

ISBN – 9789948761754 – (Paperback)
ISBN – 9789948761761 – (E-Book)

Application Number: MC-10-01-2002274
Age Classification: E

The age group that matches the content of the books has been classified according to the age classification system issued by the UAE Media Council.

First Published 2024
AUSTIN MACAULEY PUBLISHERS FZE
Sharjah Publishing City
P.O Box [519201]
Sharjah, UAE
www.austinmacauley.ae
+971 655 95 202

Thank you to my family and friends for the unconditional belief
in me.

Thank you to my educators, directors, and colleagues. I've
learnt a lot from you.

Table of Contents

بسم الله الرحمن الرحيم

Prophet Muhammad (ﷺ) said, "*Allah loves that when one of you accomplishes a work, that he accomplish it with mastery.*"(Narrated by Al Bayhaqi.)

A profession with a purpose is a performance that echoes, a presence that radiates, and a life of quality.

This book proposes that the ultimate purpose in a profession is to perform with *mastery*- **comprehensive knowledge or skill in a particular subject or activity,** whether it is making a cup of coffee or execute a strategic plan.

To perform with *mastery,* it not only requires having the needful skills and knowledge to perform very well, but to also embrace a combination of *core values- **the foundation of humans' compass that guides and shapes our decisions every day and** are formed throughout our nurture and learning experiences shaping what is called a* **value system.**

We can change our **values** as we move through life and the more positive ones we choose to embrace, the more we are able to efficiently apply our management concepts and skills that result in making us master what we practice on a daily basis. It is not what we do, but how well we do it.

The barista who forgets the cup holder and the extra hot milk you requested; is different than the barista who added a cup holder to the coffee, passed a tissue, remembered the extra hot milk, and smiled while wishing you a good day.

Doing what we do well will provide us a good reputation, job opportunities, good deeds, defines you from others, key to open opportunities.

The book is a collection of topics reflecting 11 core values written in a storytelling. **The values mentioned in the book are:** Accountability, Communication, Empowerment, Proactivity, Quality, Teamwork, Consistency, Resilience, Commitment, Community, Passion.

Each topic contains insights that are derived from learning experiences and the best practices of successful organizations. The topics illustrate that when we *operate from a dynamic core value system in any type of profession* one can fulfill his/her potential and perform with mastery, which consequently influence both coworkers, the organization, and the community as a whole.

In *Values of Mastery,* the stories are meant to motivate readers to make a difference that radiates beyond themselves whenever performing a task, solve a problem, make a decision, or interact with others inside as well as outside the organization.

I hope this book inspires novice to embrace a value system that makes mastery a state of mind. Also, I hope the book rejuvenates the mindsets of newly appointed leaders to reassess the core values of themselves and the existing corporate culture.

Sincerely,
Halah AlShathri

Accountability

1

Internal Protocols

"The purpose of internal protocols is to influence front-line positive etiquettes and create a sustainable culture that promotes excellent service."

– Halah AlShathri

Let me take you back to when a recently opened Saudi retail bank offered me the honor to serve as a founding partner and branch manager of its new primary ladies' branch.

The team consisted of six people I had never met. Four of the customer service representatives were inexperienced – it was their first job. The other two had experience at other organizations with different working values, norms, and standards.

With these facts in mind, I learnt that I needed to create a common foundation as a strategic approach to engage them, manage their daily performance, and help them become part of the working culture.

The foundation should be a code of specific behaviors that define our service etiquette, promote positive customer interactions, and create a sustainable culture in support of performance mastery, which I named ***Internal Protocols***.

Here are a few of the internal protocols we adhered too:

1. Smile when a client walks in.
2. Do not sit in the waiting area while there are clients in the branch.
3. Do not walk around the branch with a drink in hand.
4. Do not answer phone calls while you are serving a client.
5. Escort private segment clients to the private section rather than simply pointing out the direction.
6. Replace the phrase *"I do not know"* with *"I will ask and get back to you."*
7. Do not discuss personal issues while a client is present.
8. Do not have general conversations with co-workers while a client is present.
9. Talking behind a co-worker's back is not accepted, and any disturbing matter must be addressed among the employees concerned or with the branch manager.

For example, when gossip occurs, I immediately bring the two parties together to discuss the issue. Stopping gossip prevents conflict in the workplace.

10. When sending emails, copy two other team members' addresses in all cases related to clients. This protocol reflects respect for customers that will ensure they will always be served momentarily regardless of whether a particular employee is unavailable or absent. Other advantages include

improved access to information, streamlined processes, expedited problem-solving, enhanced teamwork, and increased client satisfaction.

Implementing ***internal protocols*** in our small working culture have benefitted the business outcomes in many ways. We were able to build a positive reputation communication between employees and customers, standardize the quality of service, increase the clients' satisfaction rate, and promote a consistent year-round performance of each team member.

Moreover, one of the unexpected benefits was high volume referrals through the word-of-mouth to family and friends.

Perhaps most importantly, what helped commit to the protocols is whenever any conflict arose, we solved it immediately, enabling the team to focus on delivering their best performance while enjoying their work.

Internal protocols can appeal to any type of organization in the service sector, whether a startup or an existing company. After all, no matter how good a product/service is good, without standards of protocols, it can be challenging to maintain customer service mastery and regulate the team's performance that are valid in making loyal customers.

On a final note, as a strategic tool, internal protocols offer a competitive advantage that provides a disciplinary guide for employees and lays the groundwork for performance mastery.

2
While You Are "Out of Office"

"Managers are responsible for building aware, knowledgeable, and confident team members who, in return, will feel accountable to deliver excellent performance."

– Halah AlShathri

Does the level of performance at your department or company differ while you are out of office? What is the quality of operations, sales, and communication while you are away?

The above questions are primary responsibilities that organizations hold managers accountable for, and the core element to drive performance mastery at all times is through streamlining the workflow within each department.

When a manager is present in the workplace and not out of office, it is more likely for some employees to perform better and their tasks fall into the right place and time. For example, employees promptly reply to emails, effectively communicate with other departments, better solve problems better, etc. However, are your employees less productive and engaged while you are absent or on leave? If your answer is yes, then work on securing workflow to ensure efficiency of performance and hands-on management year-round.

These listed steps can help in securing workflow systematically:

1. **Analyze**

   Analyze the current workflow of operations and/or services, such as the process, tasks, and timeframes.

2. **Measure**

   Measure employees' awareness and skills of the tasks processed by the department.

3. **Assess**

4. Assess the current integration of workflow among employees to identify gaps, challenges, and room for improvement.

5. **Specify**

   Specify all clients' key requirements from the department/store.

6. **Engage**

   Engage employees' in finding how to reach an efficient, fluent workflow.

7. **Design**

   Design a standard model for getting work done in a streamlined structure.

8. **Stimulate**

   Stimulate problem-solving skills: For example, use problem-solving storming techniques such as brainstorming, cause analysis, and Post-It Note facilitation, etc. Then, specify a timeframe for replying to inquiries and complains, such as an hour to three hours to solve a client's problem.

9. **Set a time frame**

Set a sufficient duration of executing daily operational processes. A time frame disciplines operations and enables a high degree of consistency in the quality of services provided to clients and throughout a department or an organization.

10. **Showcase**

Showcase the new workflow model to all employees for the objective of developing a knowledgeable team. Expose each member to the tasks and projects of his/her colleague working within the department.

11. **Delegate**

Delegate responsibilities, and not only roles. For example, when a team leader delegates his/her role to an employee, it's crucial to highlight the duties along with the authority.

It is important to realize that managers have an obligation to secure workflow and create a dynamic environment that enables employees to efficiently perform responsibilities and tasks, whether he/she is present to watch over their shoulders or not. For the same token, leaders feel responsible for creating aware, knowledgeable, and confident team members, who in return will feel accountable to deliver excellent performance and can influence their subordinates in the future.

3

Look Back Only to Learn and Never to Regret

"Writing a goal that is well defined increases the chances of accomplishing it."

– Halah AlShathri

A part of the traits that leaders adhere to are self-learning and embracing a positive mindset that perceives experiences as a source of personal growth. In view of these leadership traits, here are some practical approaches that empowers and encourage self-growth, which supports performance mastery:

Good intentions reinforce actions

When you summon positive intentions before physically moving toward a goal, it directs your efforts and subconscious mind toward manifesting results with determination.

Win with what you play best

This is an Egyptian saying I overheard one day on the radio, and that was the moment I decided to start doing what I had desired to do for so long: to become a writer. I would not be writing this book today if I had not started writing.

Writing goals

Writing a goal that is well defined increases the chances of accomplishing it because it becomes easier to recall and review your progress at year-end where it is an excellent time to reflect on ourselves and learn.

The equation of accumulation

Small achievements accumulate gradually in reaching the ultimate goal. The method is to start by breaking down a goal into small steps/milestones.

Trying and never giving up

Before Jack Ma found Alibaba Group, the Chinese Internet-based businesses, he applied for 30 different jobs that rejected him, such as KFC, where all 23 applicants were accepted except for him. Ali applied ten times to Harvard School, but they declined all his applications. Nevertheless, Ali's persistence has driven him to create a multibillion-dollar organization, which changed the wholesale industry.

Beautiful patience vs. patience

Beautiful patience is disciplining oneself to endure a situation without distress or complain, while remaining optimistic. It enables leaders to think critically and make better decisions for the organization; away from feeling anxious or enraged.

Consistency

Consistency is the habit of adhering to a pattern of behavior and attitude. A consistent leader possesses a significant influence on employees, stakeholders, and customers.

Communication

4

A Materialized Vision

"Create a materialized vision for your team that feels personal; closer to the heart and not just to the mind."

– Halah AlShathri

Shortly after I joined a new bank's founding team as a branch manager of its primary ladies' location, the management planned a soft opening date in September.

I remember the day when the furnishing work finished. My team walked into the branch that overlooked a main street in Riyadh city and started taking the plastic covers off the new furniture. I sensed a common feeling of concern among us all when we realized the challenge of establishing a new branch, then I smiled at them and said, "We will make this place so welcoming that our clients will always want to come back."

This particular branch was the second to open of all the branches in all regions, and we were assigned the highest quarterly targets for deposits, liabilities, and number of clients of all the ladies' branches kingdom-wide, with only three months left to year-end closing.

On the other hand, the bank offered competitive products and services, and hired its employees selectively.

During our first daily morning meeting, my team and I discussed the bank's vision and brainstormed to create a strategic sales plan.

I sensed their concern about the challenge of achieving our quarterly targets in a minimum amount of time, even though they tried to conceal their worry. For most of them, this was their first working experience—in a new branch of a new bank, with new products and services.

Weeks later, after we began implementing the sales plan, we were still far behind our quarterly targets and running out of time. I knew I needed to think of a better strategy to boost performance and morale of the team quickly.

Everyone needs a place away from external distractions and internal noise to quietly reflect on their decisions while thinking critically and objectively.

Thus, mine was in my office, so I stood in front of a large sunlit window, looking up at the light blue sky, to think clearly and explore new possibilities. I can still feel a thriving vision inside of me, but it seemed that it is not quite delivered to my team as I can tell through their daily emotional performance.

As I glanced at the building next door that was still under construction and the labor were slab casting, I asked myself two questions:

1. *What is missing in our strategy and business plan?*
2. *How can I better interpret the image and feelings of my own personal vision to make it easy for the team to envision and adopt it?*

That is when I thought why not create a strategic concept and named ***materialized vision***. I define materialized vision as demonstrating a concept with my own behavior to make it visible to the team so they can align their own hearts and minds with it.

Without delay, I called a meeting. I asked my team to stand next to me and look through the same window at the workers on the ground floor of the two-story building next door, and said:

"The construction team and our team have the same objective: to build something from scratch. The construction team's daily task is to build something in sequential steps according to blueprints. Ours is to build traffic, liabilities, and deposits according to targets. The bricklayers next door are implementing the owner's design vision. Our job is to implement the bank's vision of becoming the most favorable destination for banking service experience in Riyadh."

I added, *"We can only arrive at our vision by living the purpose of mastering our performance that will create a sustainable customer journey."*

To measure the effectiveness of this ***materialized vision*** strategy, we looked at it against KPIs and key business objectives. We were ecstatic when we learned that the branch had successfully reached its objectives. Later, we received numerous awards for achieving first place in liabilities, the highest number of clients, and the second-highest deposits – within the first quarter and others later.

The branch continued to be honored with more awards and was recognized by upper management as the top ladies' performer year after year. Most importantly, we not only successfully established the branch's infrastructure from scratch in a very short time, we proved to be a very welcoming place to our clients.

Other outcomes of our materialized vision included our embrace of teamwork and alignment with the organization's objectives. In addition, because of our shared understanding and clarity of purpose, objectives, and procedures, our team's level of accountability increased.

From a psychological perspective, ***if you can visualize your goal, it manifests into reality. Thus, as a leader, articulate your purpose and communicate it so your team can see it in action.*** That encourages engagement and helps your team understand their role in supporting the organization's objectives.

Find a materialized vision for your team that feels personal so they can connect with their hearts, not just their minds. One that will inspire individual performance and contribute to your organization's overall vision, mission, and objectives.

5

Like a Snowball

"The more you communicate effectively with employees, the more you promote performance mastery."

– Halah AlShathri

Businesses of all sizes function around four primary elements: finance, human resource, operations, and sales; where the engine that runs all four is a dynamic internal communication channel, which flows between organizational members of all levels.

For the most part, an active internal communication culture encourages employees to consistently demonstrate the right attitudes, behaviors, and competencies that deliver outstanding performance. Moreover, effective communication empowers employees and transfers them from doing routine tasks to achieving organizational objectives every day.

On the other hand, studies and personal experiences proved that when organizations or leaders spend little time and effort on communicating with employees, it results in an average performance and/or leakage in human resources. According to a study performed by Watson Wyatt found that "Businesses with effective communication practices were more than 50% more likely to report employee turnover levels below the industry average. An inter-company study found that differences in manager-employee communications practices were directly responsible for an 18% variation in absenteeism rates." [1]

Here are some key strategic tools to make effective internal communication a corporate cultural norm:

1. **Daily/weekly meetings**

    Committing to meet with your team develops engaged, and highly conscious members who are result-oriented. Some departments require weekly rather than daily sessions, so do what you think is most suitable for your business requirements.

2. **Weekly performance reviews**

    Includes ongoing feedback, follow-up, discipline enhancement, and tackle low performance at an early stage.

3. **Milestones**

    What is a better way to communicate with people than to celebrate an achievement? In fact, showing recognition and appreciation is vital to driving high performance.

4. **Open door policy**

    A manager's office is the one place that has the power to lift up an employee's spirits or to bring it down. Keep your office door open is an opportunity to listen to employees and to redirect their emotions and thoughts to attain organizational objectives. A manager's office can be a pool for collective ideas from employees, which can add value to projects or the business. One important note is that an open-door policy does not mean that office gossip or rumors becomes a part of what you listen to.

5. **Constructive feedback**

   Feedback is a golden channel where you can deliver so many messages that motivate, develop, control, and repair performance. Use positive or constructive feedback regularly as a tool for continuous improvement and increasing productivity.

6. **E-mail**

   The email is an essential median for communication to fastens business processes and recognizes employees' progress. For example, send a thank you note for a job well done, a motivational quote, an article, or a daily performance report.

Equally important, when you assign a new task or objective to your team, ensure that it is as clear as possible and provide lateral support through the above communication tools to enable employees' engagement.

After all, the more you communicate effectively with employees, the more you promote performance mastery. Like a snowball, the more you roll it, the bigger it grows.

6

Customers are Potential Personal Advisors

"We are in an era of a client/ company interactive relationship."

– Halah AlShathri

After all, when the workflow is well-managed, benefits can be harvested across the whole organization. For instance, efficiency, increased morale, reduce errors/cost reduction, and service mastery.

Feedback is a universal mean of communication that organizations use as a tool to collect information to engage or modify behavior and improve outcomes. Then, there are two important channels that feedback runs through. First is the internal one, where feedback takes place among employees, and second is the external one, that clients organizations collect from their clients.

However, in here, the focus will be on the external channel, being the metric that ensures whether a product/service is meeting or exceeding customers' expectations.

One example on the successful utilization of feedback happened on October 7, 2016, at Snap Inc., a billion-dollar company known as Snapchat, is a global multimedia application that allows users to take videos and pictures and can selectively watch them for 24 hours only.

Snapchat introduced a new feature called Auto Advance, but it did not appeal to its users. As posted by one user, "Unfortunately, this change made it impossible to individually choose which story to watch. Sometimes we just want to see what our close friends or family are up to – not all of our friends – and Auto Advance prevented that." [1] Two months later, Snapchat removed the new feature and replaced it with a different one that appeals to its users, as they built Story Playlist feature instead that meets the same objective of making meeting friends easier.

Uber, one of the fastest-growing businesses worldwide, is another example of a global platform operating worldwide that has an active external channel for feedback. The company collects riders' feedback right from the user-friendly application with one click on its help tab, and choose from one of the enlisted options, such as "I lost an item," "My vehicle wasn't what I expected," or "I had an issue with my fare." Uber's feedback model makes it easier for clients to communicate their messages, which helps the company perform at its highest potential.

As can be seen, there are common successful features of companies that embrace their customers' feedback and are responsive. For instance, increase in the number of users, brand awareness, innovation, and have a direct client-company relationship.

What can be learned from such successful cases is the importance of creating a culture that perceives customers as advisers who have the potential to provide the organization with valuable feedback and can easily communicate their experiences.

We are in an era of client/ company interactive relationship, and it is no longer enough to rely only on surveys and reports from the marketing or financial departments to know the succession of a product/ service.

For that, and to influence the perception of front-line employees, I came up with the approach that states *customers are potential personal advisors.*

Here are three tools that demonstrate the strategic approach for perceiving customers as potential personal advisors:

1. **A system that channels customers' feedback** – for instance:
   A. Place the contact information somewhere clear where clients can easily spot on your social media accounts and website.
   B. Set a response timeframe to clients' enquiries or complains on all company's platforms.

2. **A daily data report of customers' feedback** – record enquires, comments, and complains.

3. **A customer advisory board meeting:** initiate to meet directly with a sample of your clients to underrate their experience with the recent features, users' feedback, etc., and actualize it.

We are in an era of client/company interactive relationship, and it is no longer enough to rely only on surveys and reports from the Marketing or Financial Department to know the feedback on a product/service. There are more method further away from focus groups, for example lean management practice, communicate with clients directly in store, and activate all technological methods.

Equally important, those companies that already have an active communication channel should constantly review the effectiveness of their responses to customers' feedback and also become constantly proactive to find out about their customers experience with a product or service.

In the long run, when an organization develops a culture that embraces feedback and adopts specific practices to help use the data more effectively, it has the potential to build customer loyalty, increase sales, and reduce cost by around 20%. This perception calls for what Steve Jobs said back in 2007, "You've got to start with the customer experience and work backward to the technology." [2]

7

Can the theory of 4 Learning Styles Influence Consumer Behavior?

"Next time you meet a prospect, identify his/her dominant learning style, and communicate accordingly."

– Halah AlShathri

The theory of the four learning styles was developed by Neil Fleming in 1987 named VARK model of learning. Fleming theorized that there are four main types of learnings: visual, auditory, reading/writing, and kinaesthetic *(sensor)*. It suggests that information is processed differently from one person to another through, and that every person uses all the four styles, but there is one preferable over the rest when learning, communicating, and making decisions. Although there are debates around whether it is an applicable theory or not, many education and training sectors sometimes apply the theory in classrooms/training programs for shaping the teaching tools to best meet students' learning styles.

From what I've noticed that many sales representatives tend to rely on the visual approach only to win a favorable response from clients/prospects. For that, the four learning styles can benefit everyone that meets clients, starting from CEOs to sales representatives.

With this in mind, what if we integrate the theory of the **four learning styles** in the business sector, as a strategic approach that can enhance sales skills in both B2B and B2C to better communicate and excel in customer service? Such skills help professionals adapt to prospects' dominant learning style/styles, which can influence sales, consumers' behaviors, and decisions.

Here is an explanation of the four types and how it can be used by a sales representative at a furniture showroom to gain a favorable impression and a decisive decision by prospects.

Visual learners: They react to pictures, colors, maps, samples, and drawings. They also tend to have a loud tone of voice – the loudest among the three, and often use words like see, observe, look, imagine, and show me. To influence visual learners, start with presenting your most attractive collection and different color schemes. Display a video that illustrates the company's projects.

Auditory learners: They react to information in verbal forms, such as discussions and sounds. Also, they have a moderate tone of voice and use minimum hand gestures to focus on listening. This type of learners often use words like I'm listening, and I hear you. To influence an auditory learner, try to verbally demonstrate the features and benefits of a product. If you text this type, ask if he/she likes to receive an audio message rather than a text.

Read/Write learners: They require patience until they finish up creating their list of compared prices of multiple stores, make many visits to showrooms to with a number of new concerns and questions. The salesperson can expedite the decision making by creating a quick presentation or mood board of the selections and the data.

Kinesthetic (sensor) learners: They react to the three senses that are smell, touch, and taste. They use words like it smells like, it feels good, and I sensed.

To influence a kinesthetic learner, speak in a low/soft tone of voice, activate the senses by providing a sample that can be held and examined, mist your display room with an aromatic fragrance, and also offer all types of drinks that appeal to different people.

Next time you meet a prospect; identify his/her dominant learning style and communicate accordingly. Or else, if you are leading a team, embed the four learning styles approach in your sales plan to influence individuals' performance by further developing their communication skills and building better rapport with clients.

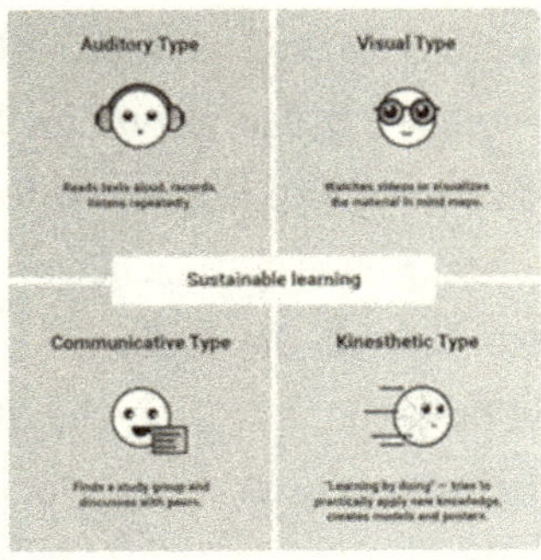

[1 To try the VARK test you can find it in their website, https://vark-learn.com/the-vark-questionnaire/

8

Redefinition of Potential and Existing Clients 2/*Every Existing Client is a Prospect*

"The information we collect on clients works as a compass that navigates the most suitable product or service to market or customize."

– Halah AlShathri

Did you just make a new client?

Congratulations, but do not rest because it is just the beginning of an infinite relationship, which you can maximize your sales. Statically speaking, "80% of future revenue will come from just 20% of your existing clients – Gartner Group." [1]

During my work at the banking industry on both service and investment sides, I noticed that some front-line employees, such as customer service, sales rep, and account managers, tend to give less attention to existing clients than when they were prospects, which results in many consequences. For example, clients no longer feel the need to retain brand loyalty, and it will result in a loss of growth opportunities.

Accordingly, I learnt that it is necessary to come up with another strategic approach for client relationship management, which states that *"every existing client is a prospect."*

The approach's objective is influencing employees to perceive every existing client as a prospect to remind us that there is still an untapped potential of needs and wants, which enables building long-lasting relationships that are financially rewarding to the organization.

In addition, acting upon the strategic approach that every existing client is a prospect stimulates the value of consistency in quality of service all over the organization, as it leaves employees with the same attitudes and behaviors they have toward prospects. Gradually, after sometime, employees will be up-to-date with existing clients' desires, buying motives, financial capabilities, and relations with competitors.

Think about it this way, when we make new friends, do we get to know everything about them on the first day? No, in fact, it takes forever because once you think you know it all, something new occurs in their lives. Thus, the same case applies to the relationship with existing clients, and the only way to know more about them is by asking questions, the right ones and at the proper time. In fact, researches indicate that asking questions is an effective tool that helps us to understand ourselves and others better.

Here are some key questions that you can ask yourself to measure the strength of your customers' relationships:

Do I know our current clients' needs and wants? Or at least 20% of clients?

Do I know if my clients have been looking for a product/service that I already provide but did not inform them about it?

Do I return phone calls and follow-up with existing clients as much as with prospects?

Do I know what type of services our clients use through competitors?

Did I directly notify clients about the new product line/service, or have I relied on the marketing campaign?

Do I know if they might have the financial capability to purchase more of our products/services?

An essential tool to influence consumer behavior and loyalty is staying attentive to the existing ones while remaining curious in them as much as when they were prospects. In the long run, the information we collect on clients works as a compass that navigates the most suitable product or service to market or customize.

On a final note, I would like to remind you of the studies which implies that it can cost around five times as much to attract a new client than to keep an existing one.

9

How Can Five Whys Get to the Root Cause of a Problem?

"Asking question has a powerful impact on solving problems in the workplace with minimum resources, anti-improving quality of services/operations."

– Halah AlShathri

Don't we all dream of having a magic wand to wave at a problem and turn it into a solution?

Sakichi Toyoda, a Japanese investor and industrialist, developed a problem-solving technique called the Five Whys, which was later used within Toyota Motor Corporation as part of the training program of its production system.

The technique's mechanism starts by first assembling a team of the involved employees, highlighting the problem, and asking a sequence of five questions that start with why, where you then turn the answer of the first question into a second why question, and so on. Once the root cause is addressed, you can decide on the appropriate corrective actions.

Taiichi Ohno, Toyota Production System engineer, explains, "The basis of Toyota's scientific approach is by repeating why five times, the nature of the problem as well as its solution becomes clear." [1]

In fact, the Five Whys technique is a magical technique that explores the cause-and-effect relationship by not relying only on logic or quick assumptions but on searching after the root cause of a problem to eradicate it once and for all and prevent reoccurrence.

Here is an example to demonstrate the five whys approach: A client complains about the late delivery of his custom-made furniture order.

1. Why is the client complaining?

The furniture arrived at the showroom after 35 days instead of 30 days.

2. Why did the furniture arrive at the showroom in 35 days instead of 30 days?

The factory delivered the furniture on the 35th day of placing the order.

3. Why was the furniture delivered on the 35th day?

The factory finished with manufacturing furniture only on the 34th day.

4. Why did the factory finish manufacturing furniture on the 34th day?

The factory's policy is that it takes 34 days for the manufacturing.

5. Why was the client not informed of our factory's policy?

The client's condition before placing the order is that it arrives within 30 days, and the sales representative confirmed just to close his deal.

Thus, the fifth answer most likely is the root cause of the problem, being a process or a system error, and sometimes it could take a sixth question or more.

In that case, the cause of problem was not due to an outrageous client, a systematic defect, or the factory's fault, but the salesperson's personal motives encouraged him to behave away from the policy. As shown, asking why five times helped in seeing through all symptoms or logic and determine the underlying cause behind the delay of delivery. However, if the real cause was not addressed, then the organization will not only misdiagnose the problem but will waste the wrong resources to solve it, and the same behavior will reoccur, causing more of customers complains.

For that, the five whys technique can be used as a strategic approach by all levels of managers, where asking question has a powerful impact on solving problems in the workplace with minimum resources and improving the quality of services/operations.

With regards to approaching problems using the five whys, Eric Schmidt, CEO of Google, said on the important practice of asking questions as a successful approach, "We run this company on questions, not answers." [2]

I leave you with two quick questions: Have you ever tried the Five Whys in solving a problem? Or do you use another method to find the obscure origin of a problem?

10
The Interrelation Between Profits and Perceived Value

"It is crucial for companies of all sizes to touch base with clients and collect feedback before making a decision related to its products or services."

– Halah AlShathri

The term perceived value defines the ability of a product/ service to satisfy clients' requirements, and not necessarily the amount on a price tag or the actual cost of production.

In 2011, customers of Netflix, the American entertainment company specialized in online streaming media, rebelled when the company announced a new strategic decision of separating between DVD mail service and on-demand streaming plans, while raising prices up to 60 percent. Customers reacted with outrage; as Reed Hastings, Netflix CEO, reported, "Netflix stock tanked as 800,0000 subscribers fled." [1]

To remedy this, Reed Hastings started by publicly admitting that he made a mistake of misunderstanding what customers wanted. Not only did Netflix hold itself accountable for its own decisions but also made a decisive redirection of its strategy by redefining the organization's business from the customers' perspective. To understand users' values, Netflix used its resources to find answers to the questions, what, when, where, and how customers watch on-demand videos. After utilizing the findings, Netflix made some changes by fixing pricing policy, enhancing services, and content with proprietary entertainment.

According to Netflix, the results were a remarkable financial success, as they were able to drive revenue and increase market share among enormous digital competitors such as Apple and Amazon.

Keeping in touch with customers is a competitive advantage and an opportunity to speculate market needs. It is crucial for organizations of all sizes to touch base with clients and collect feedback before making a decision related to their products or services, whether it is a technical or non-technical feature. Moreover, leaders should consider various channels of communication with clients, even if they believe that the new changes will be a home-run to the organization.

There are other aspects that reflect the interrelation between perceived values and profits, like when consumers understand a product's quality, the value increases in their minds. For instance, when people watch a video that shows the manufacturing process of an item, they will have a better understanding of the quality, materials used, efforts, etc., in production. Thus, such aspect can influence clients to purchase this particular product over competitors.

After all, people will listen to what you offer and assess how your products or services can make their lives better and easier in exchange to their money and time. Therefore, creating value to consumers is the master key to influence organizational growth.

Empowerment

11

Unleash the Power of People

"The value of empowerment is far greater than the power of centralization."

– Halah AlShathri

The business dictionary defines empowerment as "a management practice of sharing information, rewards, and power with employees so that they can take initiative and make decisions to solve problems and improve service and performance." [1]

During one day, a customer service representative was transferred to work temporarily in my branch as I was told that she was frequently reported by her manager with an unsatisfied performance, especially that our team was honored with the responsibility to train newcomers for most of the newly opened branches in the Central region along with the first team hired in the Eastern region.

To begin with, I met with the employee to assess her capabilities, knowledge, and experience in the field. While listening carefully and asking several questions, I was surprised to find out that she had experience working as a customer service, and had developed many supervisory competencies, which does not explain her current poor performance.

In the first place, I monitored the employee's performance for some time, then I decided to empower her by adding a few daily supervisory responsibilities and tasks while making sure that she was getting all the required support from my team to deliver as expected. Under those circumstances, the results were fascinating, as her performance was high and she added so much value to the team. Moreover, after temporarily unleashing her power, she carried more responsibilities, served clients better, and was willing to learn and handle new responsibilities. Later on, I nominated her for a supervisory role, which she earned, and later on she added value to the organization.

As can be seen, managers who are reluctant to empower their employees miss out on many advantages for both organizational and employee's growth. Although the value of being empowered varies across cultures, and the domains of a person's life, but most importantly, it capitalizes on strengths, and elevates performance.

Here are some essential strategic approaches to create an empowering environment that unleashes the power of people:

- **Organizational learning** Provide subordinates with the chance to engage in an ambiance that has shared knowledge and learning to unleash their abilities.
- **Keep employees in the loop** Inform employees of any changes within the department/organization as well as seek their opinions.

- **Make information accessible** Direct employees to resources of information that can support their daily tasks or projects rather than seem careless or reluctant to help out.
- **Recognition and ownership** To increase self-esteem, reward a job well-done in front of teammates and upper management, like sending an email with a copy to the team. Also, give credit to good ideas because that helps employees to capitalize on their efforts to meet the assigned objectives.
  Instant feedback: Provide instant feedback, whether it is positive or constructive. In fact, immediate feedback is an affirmation that leads to favorable behaviors.
- **Make leaders, not followers** Think about eating the whole pie and not only a slice. If you create leaders, it means you are adding new skills and competencies to your team, which will result in higher performance and financial returns.

The value of empowerment is far greater than the power of centralization because people are an organization's most reliable asset who build its customers' database required to make sustainable profits and growth. Therefore, seek to create an environment of cycled empowerment, where your actions influence employees to empower each other as well.

Proactive

12

Always Be Closing

"Following a closing sales strategy minimizes the gap between opportunity and luck."

– Halah AlShathri

A sales process goes through several stages that are suggested by experts, but everyone strives to reach the last stage, which is closing a sale. However, whether involved in any of the two types of business, Business-to- business, a transaction conducted between one company and another, or Business-to- client, selling a product/service directly to a client, both types require strategic approaches to close a sale.

Freelancers, relationship managers, and sales representatives strive to close deals every day and achieve that peak moment of joy; yet, they naturally experience plenty of unsuccessful attempts to make a closing.

Here is an action plan that consists of several strategic approaches to increase the chances of closing deals:

1. **Build rapport**: When you nurture a prospect to captivate his/her attention rather than presenting the products immediately, you can build the

infrastructure to close a sale. Building a rapport requires a positive attitude that must go on until the deal is sealed.

2. **Eliminate**: Stay focused on what a prospect needs. Elimination helps in tailoring products/services to the needs and value of his/her interests, which makes the decision easier and less time-consuming. HubSpot conducted a sales perception survey on how to improve the sales experience according to buyers, found that (69%) responded as "Listen to our needs." [1]

3. **Ask questions**: By asking a question like, does it solve your problem? This approach surfaces people's desires, while it can address any doubts and a method to understand what the client most values.

4. **Solve problems:** Be the solution to your client's problems and never the obstacle.

For example, on a Thursday afternoon, I received a call from a client living in Kuwait who told me that the deal is not closed due to the company's payment policy. The payment policy was 50% down payment before purchase, and the prospect could not comply with it because it will take three days util the transferred amount is credited in our account. Thus, if she the company does not start manufacturing her order, she will not be able to deliver it in five days and lose a big deal. After asking the client several questions, we came up with a solution that ensures both sides close the deal.

The solution that was proposed is to transfer the due amount and send a copy of the transaction as a confirmation, which we will act upon as a validated payment within 3 days only, then the was closed for the favor of our company.

5. **Follow-up**: To close a sale is a wish that can only come true if you follow up after the prospect's visit. Following up should start after one week of the prospect's visit and not later than that e.g., via phone and/or email. Research shows that "80% of potential opportunities are lost without trace simply due to a lack of follow-up." [2]

6. **Respond**: It is an important step in closing a deal, because responding to a call or email reflects an employee's commitment, professionalism, and the expected level of service in the future. Otherwise, a late response or not responding will draw a negative perception that discourages prospects from converting into customers.

7. **Leave an impression**: When a deal is not closed for any reason, keep your smile on and accept the prospect's decision. Thus, you reinforce the rapport and make a positive impression to remember you on the next deal or purchase.

There is another critical aspect that can influence closing a deal, and it is to ensure that employees at all levels of the organization represent its products/services with competence. For example, if the call center representative does not provide quality service over the phone, the prospect will most likely lose interest in visiting the store; hence, the opportunity to attain a new client ends before it even starts. This aspect can be achieved by ongoing feedback, training, and updates of new releases.

Although some challenges can prevent closing a sale, like a competing product or price, but that's all right; most importantly, following a closing sales strategy minimizes the gap between opportunity and luck.

13

Redefinition of Potential & Existing Clients/

Everyone is a Potential Client

"A turning point will occur when individuals and organizations perceive walk-ins/prospects as a pool of opportunities that can increase the number of new clients and closed sales per day."

– Halah AlShathri

Prospects are potential clients who either walk into your store, post an enquiry on your social media account, or contact you via email/phone call. and can end up making a poor judgment.

With regards to walk-ins, what I witnessed is that many front-line employees in different industries tend to label them according to appearance, such as bag, shoes, watch, car brand, etc.

In that case when employees make assumptions based on appearance, they become selective in the quality of service they provide and do not deliver proper behavior, hence, losing the opportunity to make a positive first impression while harming the organization's reputation. Moreover, what if the prospect was a potential buyer? Then your opportunity to make a client has just gone out of the window, and with other countless ones!

For this reason, I learnt that it is necessary to come up with a strategic approach to relationship management, which is, *"Everyone is a potential client, and every existing client is a prospect."*

Here are some approaches that elaborate on the first strategic part during my work; everyone is a potential client:

Make the first impression

Everyone that walks in deserves a proper greeting, which combines a smile and eye contact while introducing yourself.

Shine through your strengths

Everyone that enters only to enquire must have a briefing on the bank's differentiated products/services, because they consume little of the visitors' valuable time, are easy to remember, and usually tempting.

Show courtesy

If a walk-in shows interest by asking more questions, introduce her to the branch/store manager before she walks out, which leaves the prospect with a memorable impression.

Honor a client's decision

If you close a deal, such as opening an account or selling a product/service, call the branch/store manager to introduce the new client. This tactic reflects hospitality and conveys a strong feeling of appreciation and importance.

You are an educator

Educate prospects with valuable information about your products/services, like their origin, benefits, usages, etc. Educating eases decision-making and an indirect form of marketing that increases trust and engagement.

Build multiple rapports

A potential client should be introduced to a second employee, including the direct manager.

Make it easy to find you

Hand in the business card/contact info to walk-ins before they walk away, because it is the seed for growing a network's list and builds reputation in your industry.

That is to say, interpersonal aspects are essential for acquiring customers. In a nutshell, a turning point will occur when individuals and organizations perceive walk-ins/prospects as a pool of opportunities that can increase the number of new clients and closed sales per day. Thus, promoting a customer-centric culture in the organization is a tool that influences employees to consistently provide a positive experience before and after the sale.

14

Create Policies and Procedures

"Whether it is a startup or a mature company, the creation of a Policies and Procedures' manual is imperative to drive performance and growth."

– Halah AlShathri

Whether it is a startup or a mature business, the creation of a Policies and Procedures' manual (P&P) is imperative to drive performance and growth. The policy and procedure manual works as a medium to document the rules an organization enforces to shape the desired corporate culture and processes that best optimize its operations.

Companies use policies and procedures as a strategic approach to govern organizations to outline the framework that directs employees' behaviors and channels operations for achieving organizational objectives. Second, it paves the way for growth, sustainability, and customers' satisfaction.

They are aware of the fact that when lacking a documented policies and procedures it becomes both an internal and external threat that makes them prone to an increased operating cost, many human errors, financial leakage, and a high turnover.

However, having a policies and procedure manual that is written and filed on the shelves only, is not enough for creating a competitive advantage, as there is one more step that is necessary, and it is automation. Automating policies and procedure will improve the efficiency, and quality by making the processes easier for employees to adhere to, and for the company to reduce compliance cost, while creating a valuable competitive advantage.

Why is having policies and procedures crucial to an organization's sustainability and growth?

1. A tool for creating the value of accountability and resilience in an organization to achieve performance mastery.
2. Automation of P&P escalates business growth.
3. A reference for employees' that provides a clear and shared understanding among employees of the organization's values and expectations of how work is done.
4. A tool to operational excellence that defines the structure, streamlines the organization's daily operations.
5. Promotes consistency in operations, processes, and productivity across the organization.
6. Promotes quality in work environment, operations, processes, and customer service.
7. A baseline to many of employees' decisions that will be exercised in the present, and future.
8. Prevents loses, minimizes risks, and increases efficiency in individual performance, operations, etc.

9. Reflects a company's commitment to effective risk management, and compliance.

As seen, policies and procedures are an infrastructure for performance mastery and expansion in services and operations to organizations of all sizes. Needless to say, it is important for leaders to be proactive in instituting policies and procedures to an organization's new requirements or market changes.

For example, coping with the pandemic out-break was at first a nightmare challenge for many organizations in adjusting to remote-work while keeping up with the same efficiency and productivity levels. As CEO of Distribute Consulting, in an interview with Insider said, "*Unfortunately, it's not that simple. In fact, when the correct policies and procedures are not created to support off-site employees, terrible consequences are likely to occur.*" Where now many companies changed their attendance policies permanently by adding a new policy under the title: Remote work.

Leaders who create a culture that processes within a policies and processes framework not only increase employees' satisfaction rate, but also deliver value to customers and stakeholders on a regular basis.

15
Crisis Management / Pre crisis

"A pre-crisis plan provides upper management with the luxury of time to minimize risks that can make a company vulnerable during crisis."

– Halah AlShathri

On February 3, 2017, a cyber-crisis occurred when Shamoon attacked some national organizations in Saudi Arabia. Candid Wueest, the security analyst and researcher at Symantec, stated that Shamoon "renders the computer unusable by overriding the hard disk with garbage." [1] Once the PC screens turned black with typed coding, panic dominated entire organizations, but someone had to snap out of it and adequately respond to the crisis to minimize damage. According to some news reports, the IT department instantly appeared at every office and pulled out the plugs off the sockets to shut down PCs and secured the remaining information on servers.

Although I searched the pre-crisis and response plans, I was not able to have access to any, if there were some. However, there were few indications, such as the expedited response by the cybersecurity team, the announced alert by Computer Emergency Response, and the text messages sent by the Ministry of Interior, Abshir program, to their registered citizens, which state that their accounts were secured.

Such emergency situations reveal the fact that when a crisis breaks out, there is a lot to think of in limited time, and many distractions occur, such as stakeholders' panic and media coverage that can place an organization under the spotlight in no time.

The first thing to remember is that organizations of all sizes are prone to crisis, and it could occur in a project, department, and product; where it threatens the overall entity, and reputation. In that case, if senior management neglects to prepare in advance a crisis plan, it will fall into a crisis struggle, and the consequences can roughly affect the interior and exterior sides of an organization.

For this reason, crisis management was found as a strategic approach that introduces itself as the backbone for emergency situations, and it consists of three planning stages: pre-crisis, crisis response, and post-crisis. Hence, being prepared is part of the pre-crisis plan, and it is the first step in effective crisis management, which prior integrates the crisis plan into the management's structure.

The following is a brief on two elements of pre-crisis plan that organizations implement to handle a crisis before it erupts:

1. Scanning the corporate environment for any potential crisis

Scan the corporate environment, then categorize the risks from low, medium, to high. Next, identify the time-sensitive functions in policies, procedures, and operations. The final step is proposing suggested solutions and action plans to management. Such as, a scan report that is usually available in the risk register by the Risk and Control Self-Assessment (RCSA) exercise at mature sized corporations.

2. **Business Continuity Plan: Consists of five parts:**

A. **Crisis Management team (CMT)**: Form a group from different department heads to prepare the plan and execute it. Conduct a training program that assesses the team's readiness in responding to a crisis. At this stage, think of the backup resources; as Michael Watkins says in his HBS article, "Creating a centralized parallel organization, in which the leader has a designated deputy and they, too, have a backup who would take command if the others were unavailable or disabled." [2]

B. **Communication Plan:** The objective of the communication plan is to respond promptly and accurately within a framework during a crisis. First, identify clear communication channels and matrixes. Second, assign a group from the crisis management team to become the official communicator of all messages sent to the chairman, employees, clients, and media. Last, ensure that all channels are active and continuously monitor your social media platforms.

C. **IT Crisis Management Plan**: Create a secured technical plan that is crucial and not becomes a part of the organization's infrastructure required to control, access, and manage privileged accounts.

D. **Recovery sight**: Provide the required recovery equipment, systems, and locations that fully function when the unsecured or damaged ones are out of reach.

E. **Testing**: Test every department's recovery plan on a regular basis, such as the crisis team, employees, and backup systems that include premises, IT, a recovery site, etc. In addition, some organizations initiate a crisis test by creating a fake scenario that includes a role play to assess and train employees.

As seen, the approach to cyber protection, or any other crisis, should follow a strategic horizontal scan that covers all organizational angles. It is important to note that every organization defines the parameters of a crisis differently, where some think cyber security is the only alert and others expand to include crisis in operations, skewed management values, management misconduct, and smoldering.

A pre-crisis plan provides upper management with the luxury of time to minimize risks that can make a company vulnerable during a crisis, and also helps control the high costs of predicted damages. In addition, an organization that develops a pre-crisis plan has the potential to position itself positively in public, uncover opportunities, recover hard times quickly, and sustain its performance.

In short, a pre-crisis plan acts as a life buoy to a company's assets and resources.

Quality

16

The 30 Elements of Value

"Adding elements of values to your products/services that fulfill active roles in customers' lives can drive financial growth and attain customers' 'loyalty.'"

– Halah AlShathri

Leaders who believe that perceived values – what consumers are willing to pay for – have as much impact on growth and sustainability on the business as pricing and marketing do, will have a higher potential to gain loyal customers and create brands with a competitive advantage.

In a Harvard Business Review published in September 2016, the researchers Eric Almquist, John Senior Nicolas, and Bloch introduced a new model called the 30 Elements of Value (EOV). The model addresses four categories of basic consumers' needs: functional; emotional; life changing; and social impact, where each one is fulfilled through a specified thirty elements of value.

The EOV model's objective is to serve commercial purposes by enabling organizations to identify consumers' needs and to deliver more elements of value through their products and services.

As can been seen below are The Elements of Value model: [1]

The tormenta of value pyramid

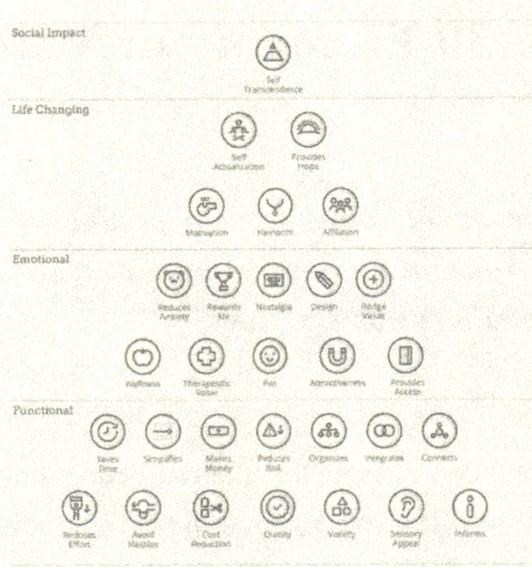

Another key point is that the researchers have done a survey on more than 10,000 US consumers' perception from around 50 US-based companies only to test the relevance of EOV. The first hypothesis is that companies who strategically integrate multiple elements of values to a product/service, have more loyal clients than the rest of competitors. The second hypothesis is that companies who add four or more values to a product/service have an increased financial return at a much faster rate than others who add three elements and less.

Other research analysis finding states that companies that achieved multiple functional elements have increased their market growth rate. For example, Amazon Prime service started with several functional elements such as reducing cost and saving time while continuously adding additional ones until it penetrated 40% of the US retail market share by 2015.

For example, CVS Health found out that their clients' needs fall within the functional and emotional categories, such as the values of providing access and wellness. Therefore, CVS Health bought Target's pharmacies to add over 1,600 locations in 47 states to provide accessible locations to clients. The company also created the Minute Clinics to provide various medical and wellness services, like general exams, vaccinations, etc.

Here is a summary of a few strategic approaches suggested by the researchers to guide leaders on how the Elements of Value model can thrive organizational performance.

1. Spend more time with customers to understand what they value most.
2. Use the four categories in the hierarchy and apply a mix of values within your products/services to meet multiple clients' needs.
3. Collect clients' feedback on the new product/service features and modify if needed.

When referring to the elements of value model as a guide in designing or developing products and services, it will enable you to add features that fulfill active roles in customers' lives, which can increase sales, drive financial growth, enhance customers' experience and loyalty. Needless to say, there is one element that no other can replace, and must manifest within every product or service – the value of quality.

17

Utilization of Customer Service Quality (CSQ)

"One benefit of integrating quality as a value in all processes is being customer centric."

– Halah AlShathri

One day a businesswoman walked into a showroom to shop for a dining set, but there was not an available quantity for her catering event. The salesman informed her that there are more available pieces at the company's primary storage; however, they will be available in the showroom after four days. The client expressed her strong desire to receive the items sooner because she wants to use them by next week for an upcoming event.

Four days passed and the items had not arrived at the showroom due to a delay from the inventory. The salesman waited another day, but when the products and the items had not arrived, the client reacted negatively to her "unmet promises and average service," as she stated.

Later, while analyzing the problem, I found out that, first, the storage was facing technical problems that prevented him from proceeding with the delivery, which was not an accepted reason. However, despite the technical issues that could have been handled better, the primary concern at this stage was the client. Thus, the second issue was that the sales representative did not make any attempt to complete the customer experience with quality and at least meet the client's expectations. Therefore, to avoid any further delay, the next day, the sales manager was asked to drive all the way to collect the items from storage and bring them back to the showroom.

The root cause was that the sales representative did not embrace the value of Quality Customer Service (CSQ), as well as not properly employing the company's resources to support services and sales.

What some companies fall short of is to embrace a framework for service quality and also to include problem-solving as a competency in key performance indicators (KPIs) as tools to enhance efficiency in the workplace throughout all departments. Thereby, after addressing the cause, it was important to realize that there is a direct correlation between the quality of customer service and the satisfaction rate.

To narrow the gap between quality of customer service and satisfaction, here are three fundamental strategic approaches to help integrate the value of quality within the organizational system and optimize efficiency:

1. **Create a customer experience:** For example, due to Apple's consistency at the in-store customers' experience at every location around the world, it established a strong brand identity. The experience includes an employee greeting you at the door while carrying an iPad in his/her hands and checking in to

see if you have an appointment at the Genius Bar. There are a number of employees in the showroom standing around the products' display table, ready to answer general questions. Finally, you get to check out from wherever you are standing in the showroom.

2. **Create a timeline procedure:** The timeline is for solving clients' problems and complains. For example, the operational strategy of solving clients' problems must be divided into several steps for each issue, spread each one on a timeline, a certain number of days from beginning to closing, specify the reporting line, and allocate available resources that can.

3. **Set weekly review meetings:** Commit to review the clients' solved problems/ complains against employees' feedback to have control over the quality of service and for continuous improvement.

Hence, for off-line or online stores in any industry, one benefit of integrating quality as a value in all processes is being customer-centric, which stimulates satisfaction rate, fosters loyalty, and results in building a sustainable competitive advantage to an organization.

I leave you with two questions to think about: Are you encouraging your employees to be problem solvers or service providers only? Are your employees aware of the company's existing resources that can increase the quality of service?

18

Quality of Service in a Town Hoping for a Tourism Revival

"To become an influential leader, have a principle, commit to it for better or worse, and embrace your employee during thick and thin times."

– Halah AlShathri

My family and I spent 2016 spring break in, Sharm El Sheikh, Egypt. For the past year, the city has experienced a drastic drop in tourism due to a Russian jet that crashed in Egypt. When the tourism industry accounts for 30% of Egypt's economy, some hotels have shut down due to a lack of demand, and others have sent many of the resorts' staff on unpaid leave.

Many tourists directed their destinations to different countries until later. As a consequence, the hotels in the city of Sharm El Sheikh have marked down their prices to cope with the crisis, varying from 10% at The Four Seasons Hotel and Resorts to 40% or more at other hotels.

We chose to stay at the Four Seasons Resort, Sharm El Sheikh, for the second time. The Four Seasons Hotels and Resorts had established its place as one of the best, if not the best, in the hospitality industry. We found out that the hotel was less than 50% occupied, not to mention that the staff's no basic salaries were relevant to the occupancy of the hotel! Only a few employees were working because they were sent to other active locations in different countries or given the option to take three months' unpaid leave until the tourism industry revives. However, what was great about the hotel is their priority not to fire an employee.

I noticed that we had the same exquisite experience that we had three years before, which was in a thriving tourism industry. During my stay at the resort, I wrote a daily journal of the practices that reflected well-managed employees during a crisis. I noticed that we had the same experience that we had three years before, which was when much better political conditions prevailed.

Some of the best practices maintained by The Four Seasons Hotel and Resort at Sharm El Shiekh during the tourism crisis are:

Positive attitudes

All staff, with no exception, carried positive emotions reflected in their body language and tone of voice during all day.

Service, service, service, oriented

For example, if you ask a non-restaurant staff about a specific meal cooked in the hotel's restaurant, expect two things: He either has the answer, or he would pick up the phone, dial the restaurant, and ask them for the answer.

You would never hear the answer "No" or "Not available."

For example, if you ask for a product they don't carry with their amenities, they either have a procedure to make it available for you or they would find a way to provide it for you.

High spirits

For example, my brother called up the golf car extension number and said in a joking voice, "Excuse me, I'd like to have a helicopter to pick me up from my room."

Employee: "Sir, you don't have a helicopter landing spot."

My brother: "It's OK, please land right in front of my room."

Employee: "OK, right away, sir!" He did arrive, but with a golf car, of course. What interested me most is how the employee and other ones are high-spirited and interactive during such circumstances.

To wrap up my observations, I researched on the core values of The Four Seasons Hotels and Resorts, where I found that their first and ultimate principle of its corporate culture is summarized in the following statement: "In all our interactions with our guests, customers, business associates, and colleagues, we seek to deal with others as we would have them deal with us." [1] They choose their employees carefully after five interviews, meet their employees' needs and wants, and treat them fairly.

The challenge facing both hotel management and employees during that crisis is to maintain the principles, quality of service, and employees' positive attitude to deliver excellent performance every hour of the day.

Despite the drastic drop in tourism, the Four Seasons Resort, Sharm El Sheikh, was able to adapt to the crisis to the point that their guests would like to return back for next spring break.

To become an influential business leader, have a principle, commit to it for better or worse, and embrace your employees during thick and thin times. As a consequence, you will be able to build a culture with sustainable performance mastery and brand loyalty.

19

What Can We Learn from a Korean Automobile Industry?

"Embrace quality as a core value and measure it."
– Halah AlShathri

Hyundai's and Kia's – a multinational automaker headquartered in Seoul, grouped in 1998 and was named The Hyundai Kia Automotive Group, referred to as Hyundai Motor Company. The collaboration happened when Hyundai owned 33.88% of Kia Motors after it announced bankruptcy in 1997. Nevertheless, both companies were experiencing a hard time in the US market due to several factors, such as failure in quality measurement.

Later in 2015, a study was conducted by J.D. Power and Associates, an automotive research firm conducts an initial quality study that measures the number of faults in the first 90 days of ownership. The study reflected an accelerated rate of improvement by both Hyundai and Kia, who ranked among the top four in quality measurements, which never happened before. Kia reached second in quality after Porsche and Hyundai fourth after Jaguar, leaving no room for the Japanese cars up on the chart. In 2016, quality study by J.D. Power and

Associates announced that Kia ranked as first on the list, which was a new record for non-luxury brands.

In short, the strategic leap in performance from a moderate quality car maker to compete against the best brands worldwide has turned heads around. As Renee Stephens, vice president of US automotive quality at J.D. Power, said, "This is a clear shift in the quality landscape." [1]

Here is a summary of the successful strategic approaches by Hyundai Motor Group to accelerate quality improvement, from worst to first:

Embrace quality as a core value and continually measure quality performance

Hyundai regulated quality assurance into its procedures as it became part of its corporate culture. It integrated quality into performance appraisal, as it became part of the competencies' scheme. Hyundai is obsessed with research and quality measurement, where it runs a full check by taking apart the car several times to detect any faults or problems before launching.

Accept and utilize feedback

Hyundai-Kia appreciate customers' reviews and are open to criticism/suggestions.

Appoint a proficient leader from the same industry

Peter Schreyer, a former Audi automobile manufacturer, was hired as chief design officer for Hyundai-Kia. Later on, Hyundai Motor Group Luxury Brand designated Luc Donckerwolke as Lead Designer, who was the Design

Director of Volkswagen Group Bentley, Lamborghini, and Audi.

Hop on your industry's trend

Hyundai-Kia is among the pioneers of the hybrid electric vehicle.

Continuous improvement:

In 1998, the company offered a warranty on the first 10-year/10,000 miles in the United States, and Hyundai experienced a sales increase of 82% during that year. Moreover, Hyundai-Kia are among the pioneers who believed that a small car should look more luxurious. Therefore, they changed the cars' designs to look more stylish and attractive.

I leave you with one thought to think of: *How can the listed strategies of quality enforcement integrate into your organization to drive growth and performance mastery?*

Teamwork

20

Why Teamwork?

"Although individualism is required in the workplace, but the lack of teamwork strategies will result in decrease of morale and productivity."

– Halah AlShathri

From early on, human nature tends to become social as people like to share experiences together, achieve basic life needs, and make mutual decisions. This kind of nature remains the same in the working environment, where there are two approaches to getting a job well done: either individually or assemble a team for it.

However, although individualism is required in the workplace, but the lack of teamwork strategies will result in a decrease of morale and productivity, which will become an obstacle in achieving organizational objectives.

With such disadvantages in mind, many great leaders promote workplace collaboration as a key success factor in business, such as Steve Jobs, Chairman, CEO, and co-founder of Apple Inc., says, *"Great things in business are never done by one person. They're done by a team of people."* [1]

In fact, researchers found a direct correlation between the value of teamwork and individual performance; a work environment that urges collaboration achieves higher productivity and satisfaction.

Here is a breakdown that demonstrates the crucial influence of teamwork on a personal, organizational, and community level:

Personal level

Personal growth

Exposing individuals to a variable number of new soft and technical skills through their teammates that enhance their performance.

Expertise

Assigning tasks of the same project among team members will give a chance for each one to concentrate and increase knowledge. Thus, the organization/department will utilize that knowledge in executing that project and other future ones.

Develop emotional intelligence skills

Being part of a team requires a fair amount of emotional intelligence, respect, valuing different opinions, and maintaining relationships, for instance, interpersonal communication skills.

Organizational level

Cross training

There are many benefits to cross-training on the organization. For instance, the workflow will not be affected during the absence of an employee, and the efficiency of individual performance increases.

Higher efficiency

When more than one person assesses a project, the company has a better perspective and evaluation, as well as a higher potential to detect errors.

Diversity

An excellent opportunity to explore a diverse number of solutions, ideas, and perspectives that can develop the organization's performance.

Streamline operations

To streamline the operations of a project/department and employees can efficiently deliver tasks, employees have to collaborate and are not out for themselves.

Community level

Advocate

Team players are advocates who promote the values of teamwork among their circles and can raise awareness of its significance outside of the organization's doors.

Giving

A study by the Academy of Management Journal by Jasmine Hu, "*An analysis of 67 different teams working at six different companies found that employees excel when they feel their work will help their colleagues, customers, and community.*" [2]

If you are convinced of the importance of teamwork in fostering commitment, development, and growth, consider the strategic approach to demand it as a critical skill for the job and also a part of the competencies in key performance indicators (KPI), which will result in many associated factors such as aligning individual performance with organizational objectives and decreasing turnover while retaining talents.

96

21
From SWOT Analysis to Strategic Planning

"SWOT analysis is designed to help re-identify the company's current situation to influence its future."
– Halah AlShathri

The SWOT analysis is a strategic tool consisting of four quadrants: strengths, weaknesses, opportunities, and threats, which is designed to help objectively define the company's current situation in order to guide its future.

Strengths and weakness identify what a company does well or poorly and include **internal** factors like financials, physical resources, past experiences, culture, products/ services, and the brand name.

Opportunities and threats are the **external** influences that exist in the environment or community and impact the company's favorable and unfavorable circumstances. Those external factors include the economy, technology, industry trends, demographic changes, and competitive advantages/ disadvantages.

We used SWOT during the planning stage of the branch's first opening to analyze our internal and external influencing factors.

Here is a partial glimpse of the branch's SWOT breakdown, showing the factors that helped it create its strategic sales plan:

Strengths

Competitive advantage:
Two differentiated services and one product.
Physical resources:
Upscale location at an intersection of two prominent roads.
Human resources:
30% of staff have five years of experience or more.

Weaknesses

Human resources: 50% of staff are fresh graduates with little work experience.
No media coverage or promotions supported the launch.

Opportunities

Competitors: Several banks are located on the same street, and our targeted prospects will be able to see the new branch while they drive through the area.

Economy: a boost in governmental and commercial projects and increased cash flow.

Threats

Competitors:

We searched for promotions offered by the competing banks, and literally visited other banks in the area to measure their strengths and weaknesses in service, products, and promotions.

Economy:

A shift in local administrative spending toward non-commercial projects.

Political:

There were no political issues that might cause a threat of any kind.

After shedding light on the unknown possibilities (opportunities and threats) and the present reality (strengths and weaknesses), many potential strategic decisions were considered to guide training, sales tactics, quality of service, and other elements of the bank's planning.

The SWOT analysis framework sets the wheels of analysis and creativity in motion. It allows you to see where you can convert weaknesses into strengths and threats into opportunities, as it also challenges the team to better understand one another to enhance their communication and collaboration that will benefit both individules and the organization.

22
Strategy of Acknowledgment and Celebration

"Acknowledging employees' efforts and behaviors makes them strive to produce more and contribute to the organization's objectives."

– Halah AlShathri

Who likes to perform in a dull environment? Who would not want to overperform in an environment that acknowledges and salutes efforts, ideas, and a high performer?

For example, we spend so many hours working in closed offices and get engaged in a daily routine that lacks enthusiasm and motivation. In consequence, the projected impact should the routine not be addressed at a company is creating an average productive culture that lacks innovation and growth.

For the purpose of create a happy culture that influences productivity, integrate the two fascinating values of recognizing employees' accomplishments and celebrating occasions. In effect, acknowledging employees' efforts and behaviors makes them strive to produce more and contribute to the organization's objectives, whereas celebrating milestones gives the team a chance to bond and indulge in the project's success.

Here are a few strategic approaches of acknowledgment and celebration to embed within the organization's shared culture that encourages performance mastery:

1. The start of a meeting is always a holistic time to acknowledge both individual and team's accomplishments.
2. Pass on to employee's complaints by clients and recognitions by upper management.
3. Make the internal email a platform to regularly acknowledge individuals' efforts and announce achievements, while copying the rest of the team.
4. Make praising and motivational feedback part of your character. Such as well done, valid suggestion, excellent job, and keep up the good work.
5. Celebrate special occasions such as, meeting targets, upgrades, engagements, projects' succession, and so on. Also, celebrate small successes and milestones.

A funny example on a moment of celebration happened when I announced to my team that we ranked again as the highest deposits among ladies' branches kingdom-wide for the quarter. To my surprise, one of the ladies raised her arms in a motion that indicated joy and celebration! I instantly imitated the move to reinforce her sense of accomplishment, and the rest of the team members followed along. From there, the expressive motion comes up every time we achieved a target, whereas celebrating became a part of the team's culture and in various forms, such as a festive meal, breakfast day out, etc. As a result of that new ritual, the level of job satisfaction increased, and it spread like a virus to our clients every day.

After all, leaders have a choice to make every morning; therefore, what prevents you from choosing a positive mindset that acknowledges and celebrates the accomplishments of your workforce.

Consistency

23

Maintain the Momentum

How to maintain the team's momentum, and sustain performance mastery?

"There is a gray area in leading teams, where a manager moves from decision making and holding employees accountable; to blending in and becoming a part of the team."

– Halah AlShathri

How can a leader fulfill his/her significant role to drive productivity and sustain performance mastery?

The first and most important element is building a teamwork-based culture where employees enjoy working together every day and enabled to develop both soft and technical skills needful.

In fact, there is a gray area in leading teams where a manager moves from decision making and holding employees accountable to blending in and becoming a part of the team.

Here are several tools to strategically build a culture that promotes the value of teamwork:

1. **Vision:** Identify a clear vision to become the roadmap that directs employees toward accomplishing the organization's vision and objectives.

2. **Policies and procedures**: Write a set of policies and procedures that relate directly to the team's goals and operations, aside from the organization's P&P. Such action clarifies how you expect them to interact with their day-to-day operations.

3. **Objectives**: Set both individual and team objectives to emphasize the importance of personal contribution and encourage teamwork.

4. **Feedback**: Acknowledge both individual's and team's achievements. Be as prompt as possible in giving feedback, and never take employees' performance for granted, even if it is their job.

5. **Conflict resolution**: Resolve conflicts immediately or they will go viral.

6. **Communication**: Communicate on a regular basis with your team and individually to fulfill both needs.

7. **(KPIs):** Use key performance indicators (KPIs) to track progress on a regular basis against objectives. It is a proper process for employees to reflect personally on their performance, and it provides leaders with control to make corrections or to pivot if required.

8. **Celebration**: Reward and celebrate individual's, and the team's accomplishments.

9. **Grow your people:** Invest the time to coach and guide your employees during working hours according to each ones need.

10. **Lead by example:** Leading by example is a crucial way to earn employees' trust and become a magnet that attracts others.

Despite the organization's size, when leaders strategically turn the value of teamwork into a corporate culture norm, they will multiply productivity and create a competitive advantage.

In short, organizational leaders set the ground for an environment that nurtures employees and empowers them, because their collective efforts will help make the changes required for meeting organizational objectives.

24

Strategy and Operations vs. Building Efficient Teams

"Teams to organizations are like core muscles to a body, where both require constant strengthening for an outstanding performance."

– Halah AlShathri

Whether you currently own a company or hold a managerial role, there are two fundamental pillars of success that require attention: 1) Strategy and operations; 2) Building and managing efficient teams. The question now is, which one are you spending more time on?

For one thing, when leaders of an organization relate poor financial performance solely to strategy and operations, the findings will mostly be tangible causes such as plans, processes, technical product, and market factors. In that case, leaders could lose sight of a possible cause that is inefficiency of teams due to a lack of communication, supervision, training, empowerment, etc.

Therefore, to accomplish financial objectives, it is vital to be self-critical in managing employees and also optimize the effectiveness of people who are a major resource to the organization.

That being the case, balancing between strategic planning and operating systems and building productive teams is the strategic approach to creating a corporate culture that promotes strategic thinking, accountability, continuous improvement, and effective communication, which will maximize financial performance. Otherwise, the imbalance of attention will result in wasting efforts, increasing cost, and underperforming individuals.

Here are some questions a leader can ask to shed light on the possibility that poor financial results can sometimes be due to a lack of common values:

- Do you communicate the objectives directly to employees?
- What are the team member's positive/negative attitudes in the workplace?
- What are the three core values of each employee in the team?
- Are there any required training courses to enhance their performance? Or do they need coaching sessions?
- What are the current obstacles that employees face in the workplace?
- Do they communicate with each other respectfully?
- Do they hold themselves accountable when they cause a problem?
- Is the team leader communicating efficiently and playing a disciplinary role? How?

Leaders can tap into employees' full potential and enhance financial performance when they spend equivalent time between implementing strategy, running operations, and building efficient teams. Therefore, monitoring teams is a continuous process that should not be within a timeframe because they are the engine that executes plans and operations required to achieve organizational objectives. Teams to organizations are like core muscles to a body, where both require consistent strengthening for an optimal performance.

With this in mind, a leader should compare the percentage of time he/she spends over operating and closing deals to generate profitability versus communicating, following up, motivating, or engaging with team members.

25

Are You Building to Last?

"Visionary organizations rely on the company more than its leaders or products to stay longer in the market."

– Halah AlShathri

A success of a company is not measured by its size but by the number of years it lasts in the market and influencing its industry *through productivity and innovation.*

Collins and Porras spent six years doing a research project at the Stanford University Graduate School of Business on 18 long-lasting organizations that were founded before the 1950s and lasted more than 50 years in their industry. The research objective is to identify the common fundamental habits behind the sustainability of so-called visionary companies and compare each one with its direct competitors. Some of the companies are Disney Land, HP, Walmart, Boeing, and Sony.

The writers documented their findings in the bestseller Built to Last, which includes a survey of 1000 CEOs with multiple generations and enlists the successful habits of visionary companies. The book has sold more than 3.5 million copies worldwide and has been translated into 16 languages, presenting compelling examples based on stories and research data.

Here are two of the prominent underlying characteristics that visionary companies embrace during their growth journey: clock building, not time telling, and preserve the core/stimulate progress.

Clock building, not time telling

The authors referred to The Walt Disney as an example, which lasted for over 90 years until today. One of the findings states that Disney's success does not depend on having a charismatic leader or a great product only. However, it measures its greatest success on building the internal system that makes it last long in the market, one generation after another.

For instance, Walt Disney, the founder, has once said, "Having a great idea or being a charismatic visionary leader is 'time telling'; building a company that can prosper far beyond the presence of any single leader and through multiple product life cycles is 'clock building.'" (Jerry and James).

As Richard Schickel, who did a study and wrote a book on Walt Disney, said, "Above all, there was the ability to build, build, and build – never stop, never look back, never finish – the institution. In the last analysis, Walt Disney's greatest creation was Walt Disney (the company)." (Jerry and James).

Preserve the core/stimulate progress

The authors found that while visionary companies have a mechanism that help them commit to their core values, they also drive for progress through adopting to change, innovation, and development from within and not waiting for external forces, like the market.

In fact, visionary companies hold core values that are not only rhetorical, like ink on paper, but actionable by creating an internal system of policies and procedures to ensure they are preserved and practiced by everyone.

For example, it was not enough for Hewlett Packard to speak about its values, so called HP Way, but instituted it by integrating the philosophy into the KPIs and promotions system, "making it impossible for anyone to become a senior executive without fitting tightly into the HP Way." (Jerry and James).

Another example on preserving core values is Nordstrom. "Nordstrom did not just philosophize about fanatical customer service; it created a cult of services reinforced by tangible rewards and penalties – Nordies." (Jerry and James).

In short, a main finding of the research is that visionary organizations strategically rely on the company more than its leaders or inventions to stay longer in the market. They build the organization of a system, culture, and values that make people, multiple products life cycles, and services work accordingly, while keeping an eye on the future.

Jerry and James wrote, "The builders of visionary companies seek alignment in strategies, in tactics, in organization systems, in structure, in incentive system, in building the layout, in job design – in everything." (Jerry and James).

26

Monitor Policies and Procedures

"Monitoring policies and procedures is an ongoing activity that includes supervision, detecting gaps, and amending before or once a problem occurs."

– Halah AlShathri

As much as competing products/services, competent accountants and sales teams are fundamental elements to succeed; a well-thought-out written policy and procedure manual is a priority for the performance to organizations of all sizes. Yet, having a policy and procedure manual is just the beginning, where monitoring is the essential part of its succession.

Monitoring policies and procedures is an ongoing activity that includes supervising, detecting gaps, and amending before or once a problem occurs. In the first place, leaders are the major participants in executing policies and procedures and measure their effectiveness against business objectives, while mature organizations tend to establish a compliance team who are responsible to monitor performance against its internal rules.

For leaders to deliberately make any required adjustments accordingly, it is necessary to be aware of alerting indications.

Here are some of the indications:

Cost increase

The increase in the number of injuries, higher failure rates, or costly overruns.

Multiple assignments

When you assign two persons or more to the same role, it makes it difficult to track a process, solve a problem, and find immediate support if required.

Lack of efficiency

The increase in absenteeism and appearance of inconsistent performance.

Lack of accountability

Managers of all levels find it difficult to measure accountability. The lack of outlined measures of accountability, such as job descriptions, formal announcements, etc., leads to fog judgments based on assumptions, or an administrator's preference.

Repetitive Complaint

An increase in clients' complaints about a specific process in business; for instance, customer service and delivery timeframe.

Slow Growth

The existence of gaps in policies and procedures slows down a company's growth tremendously, while an updated one boosts productivity.

Strategic decisions

When there are strategic decisions to make, such as a new division, a new alliance, or an entry of a new brand under the company's umbrella.

Technology update

The entrance of new technology into any market has the potential to enhance operational processes, which might require some changes in a procedure.

Governmental regulations

The official announcement of new rules/regulations in the country a company operates in must be integrated within the policy and procedure, because they can either enhance or threaten the business if not followed.

Companies can benefit a lot from consistent monitoring such as, to enhance the quality of operations and services, support change management, create an environment that encourages continuous performance mastery, and it make leaders and organizations resilient to change by anticipating risks that prevents many costly errors.

On other hand, neglecting to comprehensively review policies and procedures deprives the organization from deploying its assets and resources, tackling opportunities, and control operational cost, which eventually makes it very challenging to grow.

Resilience

27

Crisis Management/ Pro Crisis

"Organizations that recover, revive, and improve fast during emergencies are the ones that embrace a proactive frame of mind rather than a solely reactive."

– Halah AlShathri

When an organization finds itself in a crisis, decision-makers are accountable to handle it in the best way they can. In fact, during a crisis, managers react differently from one another. First, some managers focus only on stopping losses. Second, others redirect employees from the sense of distress to concentrate on strategically seeking out creative solutions that not only stop losses but improve the situation and tackle opportunities.

In contrast, every organization has two sides that must be taken care of during a crisis, which are the interior and exterior. The interior includes stakeholders, employees, and finances; and the external are suppliers, customers, and reputation. Yet there is a direct relationship between the two sides, where what happens on the inside affects the outsides, and vice versa.

One example from the external side is the economic crisis, where it threatens organization existence by causing effects such as deflation, a decrease in household income and purchasing power.

Without delay, if you find yourself unprepared in the middle of a crisis and without a contingency plan, consider the following strategic approaches to handle it:

- **Advisors/Intelligence committee (a crisis plan):** Initiate a team that has the skills to create and supervise a crisis plan, ground employees, and stabilize performance throughout the crisis cycle.
- **Effective Communication**: Engage all levels of employees and stakeholders by providing insights into the situation on a daily basis to create a calm environment which encourages creative problem-solving.
- **Social media**: Keep an active presence on the company's social media accounts. Closely monitor the interactions by replying to followers right away, reacting to publicity, and keeping your clients and prospects under control.
- **Be aware of the grief stages**: It is valuable to be aware of five psychological stages of grief and be compassionate with people accordingly (denial, anger, negotiation, depression, and last is acceptance.) *"It's important to try to find ways to remain open to compassion, even when we're overtaxed,"*[1]*said Amy Gallo in her Harvard business review article.*
- **Review your finance standing point**: Closely manage your cash flow and expenses, and create a saving fund, if you have not yet, incase needed for

emergencies and/or opportunities. Minimize and/or cut costs during a crisis.

- **New product line:** Consider coming up with a new product line which could either be less expensive with additional features or targets a different market segment.

- **Utilize technology cost-effectively:** Explore all possible opportunities to minimize cost and expenses by utilizing technology. For example, capitalize on social media rather than advertising.

- **Value vs. Price**: Review not only your pricing, but your prices against the values provided to consumers. Consumers tend to become more careful in their purchasing decisions by looking after value and price altogether more in crisis.

Ultimately, individuals are likely to be in a crisis that presents a different situation every day and makes leaders take experimental decisions. An example would be the outbreak of the pandemic, which created what seems to be a worldwide turbulent commerce environment.

Overall, organizations that recover, revive, and improve faster during emergencies tend to be resilient and embrace a proactive frame of mind rather than a reactive one.

Commitment

28

Where There's a Will, There Is a Way

"Set both short and long-term goals during the 365 days."
– Halah AlShathri

The proverb where there is a will there is a way, underlines the fact that what is in our mind and heart sets are the power to achieve what we want. That proved fact should encourage us to carefully select our values and become resilient to embrace new ones which will excel our personal life and work style. Value and beliefs are not enough to attain a goal, and that is why it is important to take proactive steps.

Dr. Gail Matthews, a psychology professor at Dominican University in California, did a study over 267 participants on how workplace goals can be accomplished by writing them down, and the results are, "*More than 70 percent of the participants who sent weekly updates to a friend reported successful goal achievement (completely accomplished their goal or were more than halfway there), compared to 35 percent of those who kept their goals to themselves without writing them down.*" [1]

Here is a method of six tools that can be helpful to accomplish a goal when it is used in a sequence:

Write every single accomplishment during this year
For example, redecorating your home, a job promotion, learning a new skill, and/or a new language.

Write down your goals
Categorize your goals into various domains – spiritual, financial, health, career, relationships, and personal growth.

Set both short and long-term goals during the 365 days.
Break a long-term goal into smaller ones to progress faster and master what you do.

Remind yourself every day
For example, write your goals on Post-it notes and stick them somewhere you can see them every day.

Goals must be SMART
Specific, measurable, attainable, reasonable, and within a timeframe.

Recollect goals in your prayers
Ask of our creator to enlighten and assist you in achieving your goals.

In short, the proverb *when there is a will there is a way* reflects that once we embrace unwavering commitment and passion as part of our core values, they will become the fuel to attain any goal.

Community

29

Small Is the New Big

Can SMEs Strategize Corporate Social Responsibility?

"When companies integrate CSR within their strategy, they maximize the potential to drive business growth through increase of brand recognition, customer loyalty, and sales."
– Halah AlShathri

"A coherent corporate social responsibility strategy based on integrity, sound values, and a long-term approach offers clear business benefits to companies and a positive contribution to the well-being of society." [1] is how World Business Council for Sustainable Development defines Corporate Social Responsibility (CSR.).

The founding objective of CSR is to encourage companies to make a positive impact on the environment, economy, and stakeholders, including employees, investors, communities, etc. For example, the Western side of the world is the massive retail chain Target. Since 1946, Target has committed efforts and assets toward local and environmental support. During the past several years, Target has given five percent of its profits to local communities in support of educational programs such as book donations, field trips, partnerships, and food pantries for families.

Among many other good examples on CSR practices from the Middle East is the Al Riyadh Bank donation program, that was initiated in 2009 and takes place at the beginning of every winter season. The program encourages employees to collaborate and donate winter essentials for families in need.

In addition, studies have shown that when companies integrate CSR within their strategy, they maximize the potential to drive business growth through increase of brand recognition, customer loyalty, and sales, whilst also having a significant influence on society, environment, and economy.

However, Corporate Social Responsibility (CSR) is often associated with large size organizations, while small and medium enterprises seem to engage less in such practices for many reasons, which makes it a pool of untapped opportunities for both SMEs founders and its societies.

Here are several facts that reflect the added value of SMEs if they were to integrate corporate social responsibility into their strategic business plan:

SMEs role in the economy: SMEs are a significant contributor to the gross domestic product (GDP) of a country, with a rate that ranges from 60% to 90%.

SMEs role in the environment and society: Due to SMEs direct trading and communication with social circles in their local community, they have a broader insight and endless opportunities for social and environmental influence. Some researchers found that engagement in CSR activities could roughly cover and solve not less than 50% of the social and environmental issues in a country.

SMEs role in the community: SMEs have a significant potential to increase the employment rate when companies sell or manufacture locally.

SMEs role in the sustainability of business: People like to label themselves with a brand of a cause. Therefore, contributing to the society engages consumers, increases brand identification, and allures the attention of investors and the media.

SMEs role in employees' welfare: Researchers report that companies with social and environmental purposes become an attractive environment to work within. For instance, Nielsen Global Survey of Corporate Social Responsibility and Sustainability, 2015, Credit Suisse reported that *"millennials are most willing to pay more for products and services seen as sustainable or coming from socially and environmentally responsible companies."* [2]

It is understandable that not all small business and sectors make high profit margin, as they also tend to reinvest their returns. However, there is a good example of a Saudi micro-sized enterprise that practices CSR in a creative method. A hair growth treatment brand that manufactures natural hair treatments announces in its social media account a give away from its actual products for cases of hair loss disease due to alopecia areta.

Now that CSR has become a strategic element that is mostly adopted by large organizations; do you believe that SMEs can strategize corporate social responsibility as a value?

Passion

30
Love

"It is alright not to know yet what you are passionate about, as long as you are determined to deliver with mastery."
— Halah AlShathri

While reflecting on the sense of two phrases by an anonymous resource: Love what you do, and do what you love, I asked myself a question, "Do I love what I do?"

I also asked colleagues and friends the same question, I found common indications that can measure our love of a profession, a craft, or a hobby:

The desire to accomplish

If you find yourself willing to do the same work every day, then nurture this kind of desire, because it will lead you to continuous success.

Commitment and dedication

Assertive to the obligation of completing a project or planning for the next one regardless of the challenges that present themselves. Also, devoting yourself to do whatever it takes out of the required context only to deliver and achieve the goal.

Passion

If a current passion makes a career, then it is too good to be true, and one should hold on to it. If not, develop more skills that are required to make a career around what you are passionate about.

However, it is alright not to know yet what we are passionate about, as long as we are determined to deliver with mastery, which can eventually make us master any profession, craft, or hobby, and never want to stop.

As Kelly Bowles, director of the user experience at LinkedIn, says, *"Build happiness into your career by finding the interaction of what you love and where you excel professionally. Work doesn't feel like work when you enjoy what you're doing and see that you're making a positive difference!"* [1]

There are different factors that can affect our motives in a negative way, such as wages and the workplace environment. Moreover, although there is not a profession where we can love all its responsibilities and tasks, they are still necessary to accomplish for our sake and the stakeholders; thus, find a way to accept and enjoy them.

For that, whether an employer, employee, or a freelancer, capitalize on the fields that energize you most by self-learning to develop new skills, abilities, and knowledge to deliver at each level with the best you do.

In consequence, you will find that your commitment will influence also your performance and your social cycle around you.

This makes me reminisce about a poem by one the best-selling poets of all time, Khalil Gibran's, *Work*:

"And what is it to work with love?
It is to weave the cloth with threads drawn from your heart,
Even as if your beloved were to wear that cloth.
It is to build a house with affection,
Even as if your beloved were to dwell in that house.
It is to sow seeds with tenderness and reap the harvest with
joy,
Even as if your beloved were to eat the fruit.
It is to charge all things you fashion with a breath of your
own spirit.
Can you think of other indications of love for a profession?"
[2]

References

2. Internal protocol

1. Dr. Pamela A. Wilson, Patricia A. Berry. Leadership and the Spouse: A Guide to Mentoring: LuLu Publishing Services, 2017.

4. Like a snowball

4. Last, F. M. (Year, Month Date Published). Article title. Retrieved from URL https://yourbusiness.azcentral.com/communication-affects-productivity-statistics-27004.html

5. Unleash the power of people

1. Empowerment. BusinessDictionary.com. Retrieved November 28, 2017, from BusinessDictionary.com website: http://www.businessdictionary.com/definition/empowerment.html

6. Generating returns vs. building teams

1. Coutu, Diane. (May, 2009). Why Teams Don't Work. Retrieved from URL https://hbr.org/2009/05/why-teams-dont-work

7. Customers are potential advisors

1. Heath, Alex. (Oct 07, 2016). Snapchat just changed how you watch Stories and buried its Discover section. Retrieved from URL
https://nordic.businessinsider.com/snapchat-launches-storv-playlists-moves- discover-section-2016-10/
2. GEORGIA. (Oct 26, 2013). Snapchat just changed how you watch Stories and buried its Discover section. Retrieved from URL
https://www.imore.com/steve-jobs-you-have-start-customer-experience-and-work- backwards-technology

9. Redefine potential and existing clients – Part 2

1. MCKEOWN, KEVIN. (NOVEMBER 12, 2014,). Focus on Keeping and Growing Your Existing Clients.
Retrieved from URL
http://www.leadershipcloseup.com/2014/11/12/revenue-growth-retention-keep-grow- existing-clients/

10. Always be closing

1. HubSpot. (April 7, 2016). How to improve the sales experience, according to buyers? Retrieved from URL

https://research.hubspot.com/charts/how-to-improve-the-sales-experience-according-to-buyers?

2. Clay, Robert. Why you must follow up leads. Retrieved from URL
http://www.marketingdonut.co.uk/sales/sales-   techniques-and-negotiations/why-8-of-sales-people-get-80-of-the-sales

11. Can the theory of 3 Learning Styles Influence Consumer Behavior?
https://archive.blogs.harvard.edu/learnmegood/which-type-of-learner-are-you-and-which-learning-style-fits-you-the-best/

Policies & Procedures

https://www.nutanix.com/theforecastbynutanix/business/redefining-business-as-usual

13. The value of teamwork – part 1

1. Griggs, Brandon. M. (January 4, 2016).10 great quotes from Steve Jobs. Retrieved from URL
http://rocksolidbizdevelopment.com/ourblog/great-things-business-never-done-one-person-theyre-done-team- people/
2. MENDOZA, MARTHA. LIEDTKE, MENDOZA and MICHAEL. (Nov 18, 2015). Google searches itself to build more productive teams. Retrieved from URL
https://apnews.com/8c60341cc1da47e084b8e17e62e83c98

14. The value of teamwork – part 2

1. Mohdin, Aamna. (February 26, 2016). After years of intensive analysis, Google found the key to good teamwork is being nice. Retrieved from URL
http://qz.com/625870/after-years-of-intensive-analysis-google-discovers-the-key- to-good-teamwork-is-being-nice/

15. Quality of service in a town hoping for a tourism revival

1. Solomon, Micah. (Aug 17, 2017). Four Seasons Leader Isadore Sharp: Treat Employees Right So They Treat Customers Right. Retrieved from URL
https://www.fourseasons.com/about four seasons/service-culture/

16. How can five whys get to the root cause of a problem?

1. Courtney, Seiter. (Dec 17, 2014). The 5 Whys Process We Use to Understand the Root of Any Problem.
Retrieved from URL
https://open.buffer.com/5-whys-process/
2. CANNON, CHADWICK. (Feb 23, 2016). The Question Advantage: The Secret to Asking More Than You Answer.
Retrieved from URL
http://chadwickcannon.com/2016/02/the-question-advantage/

18. Are you building to last?

1. C. Collins, I. Porras, Jerry, James. Built to Last, Successful Habits of Visionary Companies. NY: Harper Business, 2002.
2. Preserve the core/Stimulate progress.

21. The interrelation between profits and perceived value

1. Peterson, Dave. Al Ramadan. Lochhead, Christopher (July 29, 2014). Why customers forgave Netflix. Retrieved from URL.
http://fortune.com/2014/07/29/why-customers-forgave-netflix/

23. What can we learn from a Korean industry

1. Eisenstein, Paul. A. (June, 2015). Korean Cars Surge in Quality. Retrieved
fromURL.https://www.nbcnews.com/business/autos/korean-cars-surge-quality-says-j-d-power-n377101

24. The 30 elements of value

1. SCHULZ, NIK. "The Elements of Value Pyramid." Harvard Business Review.ORG), Eric AlmquistJohn SeniorNicolas Bloch, September 2016, URL
https://hbr.org/2016/09/the-elements-of-value

25. Crisis management – pre-crisis

1. Alkhalisi, Zahraa. (January 26, 2017). Saudi Arabia warns of a new crippling cyberattack. Retrieved from URL http://money.cnn.com/2017/01/25/technology/saudi-arabia-cyberattack-warning/
2. Watkins, Michael. (Sep 30, 2002). Assessing Your Organization's Crisis Response Plans – Your Crisis Response Plan: The Ten Effective Elements. Retrieved from URL http://hbswk.hbs.edu/archive/3124.html

26. Crisis Management/ Pro Crisis

https://www.harvardbusiness.org/leading-your-team-through-a-crisis/

27. Small is the new big

1. Richard Holme, Phil Watts. (January, 2000). Corporate Social Responsibility: Making good business sense. Retrieved from URL
http://www.ceads.org.ar/downloads/Making%20good%20business%20sense.pdf
2. Saussier, Julie. (Feb 13, 2017). Millennials Drive Sustainability. Retrieved from URL
https://www.credit-suisse.com/corporate/en/articles/news-and-expertise/millennials-drive-sustainability-201702.html

29. If there is a will there is a way

1. Hyatt, Michael. (January 3, 2014). Five Reasons Why You Should Commit Your Goals to Writing. Retrieved from URL http://www.goalsleaminginstitute.com/goal-setting.html

30. LOVE

1. Iliff, Rebekah. (June 9, 2015). Seven Tips for Loving Your Career and Working with Passion. Retrieved from URL https://www.entrepreneur.com/article/247017
2. Aleph, Faena. (JULY 30, 2016). Work is Inseparable from Love: A Parable by Kahlil Gibran. Retrieved from URL http://www.faena.com/aleph/articles/work-is-inseparable-from-love-a-parable-by-kahlil-gibran/